LESOTHO 2016 HUMAN RIGHTS REPORT

EXECUTIVE SUMMARY

Lesotho is a constitutional monarchy with a democratic parliamentary government. Under the constitution, the king is head of state but does not actively participate in political activities. The prime minister is head of government and has executive authority. All major parties accepted the outcome of the February 2015 peaceful, credible, and transparent elections, and the country established its second coalition government. A Southern African Development Community (SADC) facilitation mission negotiated the snap election following clashes in August 2014 that saw then prime minister Thomas Thabane flee the country. The 2015 parliamentary elections gave no political party a majority. Pakalitha Bethuel Mosisili, the leader of the Democratic Congress (DC), which won 47 seats in the 120-member parliament, formed a seven-party, 65-seat coalition government. Despite the close election and tense environment, Thabane transferred power peacefully to Mosisili and assumed leadership of the opposition. Thabane and two other opposition leaders fled the country again in May 2015, citing concerns about their safety, and had not returned by year's end. An opposition boycott of parliament ended in February.

The extent of civilian control over security forces was unclear at year's end.

In May and June 2015, the Lesotho Defense Force (LDF) arrested more than 50 soldiers in connection with an alleged mutiny; 23 faced charges of mutiny or failure to suppress mutiny, and there were credible reports detainees were tortured. On June 25, 2015, LDF members shot and killed their former commander Maaparankoe Mahao in what the LDF characterized as an effort to arrest him in connection with the alleged mutiny. A SADC commission of inquiry was set up to investigate Mahao's killing and the circumstances that led to it. The commission found that, at a minimum, the LDF used excessive force in its effort to arrest Mahao, that detainees were tortured, that there was little evidence of mutiny, and that it was "doubtful" that Mahao was involved in a mutiny. At year's end authorities had not tried the 23 soldiers; 15 remained in prison, while the other eight were released on "open arrest," a status similar to being released on bail. All 23 still faced charges of mutiny or failure to suppress mutiny (capital crimes). The court martial convened to hear the charges against them was delayed several times. Authorities did not arrest or charge anyone in Mahao's killing, and there was no investigation of the torture of the detainees. The only commission recommendation fully implemented by year's end was the retirement of LDF Commander Tlali Kamoli, which occurred on December 1.

Torture and cruel, inhuman, or degrading treatment and punishment by LDF members, police torture, and societal abuse of women and children were the most significant human rights problems in the country.

Other human rights problems included retaliatory killings related to the local accordion music gangs; lengthy pretrial detention; long trial delays; restrictions on media freedom, including detention of journalists, and threats of libel suits and occasional violence against journalists; and official corruption. Societal abuses included stigmatization of persons with disabilities, human trafficking, discrimination against persons with HIV/AIDS, killing of elderly persons due to allegations of witchcraft, and child labor.

The government did not take steps to prosecute officials who committed abuses, whether in the security services or elsewhere in the government, although the army reportedly surrendered two soldiers implicated in a murder without political implications to police. Impunity remained a significant problem.

Section 1. Respect for the Integrity of the Person, Including Freedom from:

a. Arbitrary Deprivation of Life and other Unlawful or Politically Motivated Killings

There were credible reports members of the LDF and the Lesotho Mounted Police Service (LMPS) committed arbitrary or unlawful killings.

For example, on April 4, LDF members reportedly beat Mamoleboheng Besele with a spade, stick, and whip at Ha Molomo military base located at Lebakeng in Qacha's Nek District. The local chief had referred a domestic dispute between Mamoleboheng and her aunt to the LDF base for mediation. Mamoleboheng died as she left the camp, shortly after the beating. According to Development for Peace Education, a nongovernmental organization (NGO) that investigated the allegations, a postmortem report indicated Mamoleboheng died of injuries to the kidney and uterus. There were no arrests or prosecution in the case.

Following a June 2015 incident in which LDF members shot and killed former LDF commander Maaparankoe Mahao, the SADC commission of inquiry concluded in a report released in February that, "on a balance of probabilities," the

LDF used "excessive force" in attempting to arrest Mahao, and the evidence showed Mahao did not resist arrest, that evidence was handled improperly, and that the involvement of Mahao in a mutiny plot was doubtful. The LDF asserted he was killed in a botched attempt to arrest him on mutiny charges. At year's end authorities had not arrested, charged, or otherwise held accountable anyone for Mahao's death.

The SADC commission of inquiry also found "that some suspects of the mutiny were tortured with the view to have them confess to mutiny and implicate others. It could therefore be concluded that the alleged mutiny might be a fabrication."

b. Disappearance

There were unconfirmed reports of politically motivated disappearances.

For example, police constable Mokalekale Khetheng went missing following police questioning in March. Officials had detained him twice on allegations that he burned down the home of the officer in command of Mokhotlong Police Station. Following his second detention, he disappeared. Police claimed they questioned and released him. His family, however, in June filed a habeas corpus application against the Hlotse police. At year's end Khetheng remained missing and the habeas corpus case continued in the High Court.

c. Torture and Other Cruel, Inhuman, or Degrading Treatment or Punishment

Although the constitution and law expressly prohibit such practices, there were reports of torture and cruel, inhuman, or degrading treatment or punishment by the LDF and the LMPS. For example, on June 6, media reported soldiers guarding the 16 LDF detainees charged with mutiny who were in the maximum-security prison at the time denied the detainees food and medication in retaliation for their children's planned Father's Day march on June 19. The government denied any knowledge of the incident.

According to a prominent human rights advocacy NGO, the Transformation Resource Center (TRC), residents of Liqhobong in Butha-Buthe District organized a protest near the Liqhobong mine in March over insufficient hiring from the local community. Mine authorities called police to disperse them. On April 17, police arrested four residents involved in the protest, beat them with sticks and rifle butts, and detained them at Butha-Buthe police station for more than 48 hours. Police charged them with obstruction of normal mining operations and inciting public violence. The magistrate set the charge aside and pledged to broker an amicable solution between the mine and community.

Prison and Detention Center Conditions

Prison and jail conditions were poor due to lack of sanitation, heat, ventilation, lighting, inadequate medical care, rape by other prisoners, and overcrowding.

Physical Conditions: The prisons and jails were overcrowded. In September 2015 the UN Office on Drugs and Crime regional monitoring and evaluation officer for sub-Saharan Africa, Nthabeleng Moshoeshoe, urged the government to address the issue of overcrowding in prisons, which she said contributed to the spread of communicable diseases. During a commemoration of World Tuberculosis (TB) Day on March 30, the Ministry of Health screened 802 inmates and discovered that seven had TB and put them on treatment.

The army detained military prisoners in a maximum-security facility.

According to the Lesotho Correctional Service (LCS), 10 inmates died during the year due to illness.

Leribe correctional facility officers disciplined four inmates involved in prisoner-on-prisoner violence. The inmates lost some of their privileges.

Although prisons provided potable water, sanitation was poor, and facilities lacked bedding. During the prime minister's June 24 tour of Maseru Central Correctional Institution, he expressed concern over inmates using worn blankets and challenged the minister of justice and LCS to look into the matter, according to press accounts. Proper ventilation and heating/cooling systems did not exist, and some facilities lacked proper lighting. There were no reports of food shortages except for the denial of food to the detainees charged with mutiny. According to the NGO, The Crime Prevention, Rehabilitation, and Reintegration of Ex-prisoners Organization, food quality improved slightly during the year. All prisons had a nurse and a dispensary to attend to minor illnesses, but medical supplies were insufficient to meet prisoners' needs. Prisons lacked round-the-clock medical wards; as a result, guards confined sick prisoners to their cells from 3 p.m. to 6 a.m.

The LCS did not provide special assistance to prisoners with disabilities, who relied on voluntary assistance from other prisoners. As with many public buildings in the country, prison buildings lacked ramps, railings, and other measures facilitating physical access for prisoners with disabilities. The LCS did not have any personnel trained in sign language.

Administration: The manual recordkeeping system was outdated and inadequate, according to the LCS. On July 1, the Lesotho Correctional Service Act of 2016 came into effect. The act replaces the Basutoland Prison Proclamation of 1957 and regulates the organization's administration and discipline practices.

The Office of the Ombudsman stated it had received no complaints from prisoners during the year; however, prisoners were often unaware they could submit complaints to this office. Additionally, any complaints must go through prison authorities, and prisoners probably feared retaliation if they complained.

According to the LCS, prisoners and detainees have the right to submit complaints to judicial authorities without censorship and to request investigation of credible allegations of inhuman conditions. The LCS referred no complaints to the magistrate court during the year and did not report receiving any complaints.

Prisoners generally had reasonable access to visitors. According to families of those LDF soldiers detained on allegations of mutiny, however, visit schedules were sometimes changed or limited arbitrarily.

Independent Monitoring: The Crime Prevention, Rehabilitation, and Reintegration of Ex-prisoners Organization, and benevolent groups made up of principal chiefs, church ministers, representatives of the business community, advocates of the court, and other citizens, visited prisons to provide toiletries, food, and other items.

In June the Roman Catholic archbishop, accompanied by bishops, visited the maximum-security prison. Also in June the TRC wrote a letter to the LDF requesting access to the maximum-security prison. The LDF promised to look into the matter but, as of October, had not approved access for the TRC.

The International Committee of the Red Cross periodically visits a group of third-country nationals detained in the country but was not permitted to visit the LDF detainees accused of mutiny. The Crime Prevention, Rehabilitation, and Reintegration of Ex-Prisoners Organization was allowed to meet the LDF detainees in July, but only with a military escort. Their report was not made public.

<u>Improvements</u>: The correctional service completed renovations of a cellblock, kitchen, dining hall, and washing facilities at Leribe Prison. In addition, it completed renovations of a cellblock, kitchen, dining hall, and storage area at Thaba Tseka Prison.

d. Arbitrary Arrest or Detention

The constitution and law prohibit arbitrary arrest and detention, and the government generally observed these prohibitions. In May 2015 the High Court ruled the arrests of LDF soldiers detained in connection with the alleged mutiny were legal, although it strongly criticized the tactics used in the arrests. The courts further ruled the LDF failed to give the detainees a proper hearing on whether they should be held in prison ("close arrest") or allowed to go home pending trial ("open arrest") and therefore should be released pending trial. On April 29, the Court of Appeal set aside the High Court's earlier judgment that all detainees should be released pending trial. Fifteen LDF detainees remained in custody. In a subsequent ruling, the Court of Appeal ruled that the minister of defense has the authority to submit charges and convene a court-martial if he believes the evidence is compelling. The court did not, however, make a pronouncement on the evidence.

Role of the Police and Security Apparatus

The security forces consist of the LDF, the LMPS, National Security Service (NSS), and the LCS. The LMPS is responsible for internal security. The LDF maintains external security and is authorized to assist police when the LMPS commissioner requests aid. The NSS is an intelligence service that provides information on possible threats to internal and external security. The LDF and NSS report to the minister of defense, LMPS to the minister of police, and the LCS to the minister of justice, human rights, and the correctional service.

Civilian authorities generally maintained effective control over the LMPS, NSS, and LCS. In 2014, however, former LDF commander Tlali Kamoli defied the then prime minister (who was also minister of defense) by continuing to function as de facto LDF commander following his dismissal. In November 2014 Kamoli left the country for a leave of absence as agreed to under the Maseru Security Accord, brokered by SADC. In May 2015 the new coalition government reappointed Kamoli as LDF commander even though he had never acknowledged his dismissal. The SADC commission's report, which concerned the events that led to the death of former army commander Maaparankoe Mahao, concluded Kamoli's dismissal had been legal and that his reappointment was legal "although the manner in which it was done was flawed."

There was a general public perception the LDF and LMPS did not hold their officers accountable for abuses they committed, including killings, torture, and corruption. For example, LDF members called before the SADC commission of inquiry looking into the killing of Mahao refused to disclose the names of the soldiers involved or any operational details. The commission's report urged the government to expedite investigations into Mahao's death and other crimes allegedly perpetrated by the LDF. There were no reports of impunity involving the NSS or LCS.

The Police Complaints Authority (PCA) investigates allegations of police misconduct and abuse. The PCA was ineffective because it lacked authority to fulfill its mandate--it could investigate only cases referred to it by the police commissioner or minister for police and could act on public complaints only with their approval. The PCA also lacked authority to refer cases directly to the Prosecutor's Office. The PCA did not publish its findings or recommendations.

The Directorate on Corruption and Economic Offenses (DCEO) investigates and prosecutes cases of corruption, including police corruption, referred to it by the government or based on substantiated public complaints. DCEO officials complained of insufficient staffing and resources to investigate all complaints received. The DCEO operated only in the capital since it did not have offices in the districts.

Of 74 cases reported to the DCEO from January through August, it referred 46 to police or the Lesotho Revenue Authority and 28 were pending investigation.

Arrest Procedures and Treatment of Detainees

The law requires police, based on sufficient evidence, to obtain a warrant of arrest from a magistrate prior to making an arrest on criminal grounds. Police arrested suspects openly, informed them of their rights, and brought them before an independent judiciary. Police must inform suspects of charges upon arrest and present suspects in court within 48 hours, although at times they failed to adhere to this requirement. The law provides the right to a determination of the legality of the detention by a magistrate or judge. The law allows family members to visit inmates.

Police did not always notify families of their relative's detention and are not legally required to do so.

The law provides for bail, which authorities granted regularly and, in general, fairly. Defendants have the right to legal counsel. Authorities generally allowed detainees prompt access to a lawyer and provided lawyers for indigents in all civil and criminal cases. Free legal counsel was usually available, from either the state or an NGO. The Legal Aid Division under the Ministry of Justice and Correctional Service offered free legal assistance, but a severe lack of resources hampered the division's effectiveness and resulted in a backlog. NGOs maintained a few legal aid clinics. The law provides that authorities may not hold a suspect in custody for more than 90 days before a trial except in exceptional circumstances.

There were no reports of suspects detained incommunicado, held under house arrest, or reports of authorities ignoring court orders for their release this year.

Pretrial Detention: Pretrial detainees constituted 20 percent of the prison population. The average length of pretrial detention was 60 days, after which authorities usually released pretrial detainees on bail pending trial. Pretrial detention could last for months, however, due to judicial staffing shortages and unavailability of legal counsel.

Detainee's Ability to Challenge Lawfulness of Detention before a Court: Detainees can challenge their arrest or detention in the courts. For example, three detained LDF members filed a High Court application seeking release and permanent immunity from prosecution. They argued they were tortured at Setibing army base following their arrest and their continued detention was in contravention of the SADC commission of inquiry recommendation that they should be granted amnesty.

e. Denial of Fair Public Trial

The constitution and law provide for an independent judiciary, and the government generally respected judicial independence.

Trial Procedures

The constitution and law provide for the right to a fair and public trial without delay, and an independent judiciary generally enforced this right.

Defendants enjoy the right to a presumption of innocence. In most cases officials informed defendants promptly and in detail of the charges with free interpretation as necessary. In some cases interpreters were not readily available, resulting in postponement of charges.

In civil and criminal matters, a single judge normally hears cases. In constitutional, commercial, and appeals cases, more than one judge is assigned. Trials are open to the public. A backlog of cases in the court system delayed trials.

According to the LDF Act, a court-martial consists of the president of the court martial and at least two other members. If the maximum punishment is death, as for mutiny, the court-martial should include an additional four members. The court-martial sits in open court and in the presence of the accused, unless the accused is disruptive. A defendant may appeal a conviction by a court-martial to the Appeal Court on any ground involving a question of law, fact, or both.

Defendants have the right to be present at their trials, to consult with an attorney of their choice, to have an attorney provided by the state if indigent, and to have adequate time to prepare their case, although resources were limited. Authorities provide free interpretation as necessary during proceedings at the magistrate and High Court levels, but not at other points in the criminal justice process. By law interpretation is not mandatory at the court of appeal level. Defendants have the right to access unclassified government-held evidence. The law provides that the government may not use classified evidence against a defendant.

Defendants may confront and question witnesses against them and present witnesses on their own behalf. The law allows defendants to present evidence on their own behalf at the Magistrate Court, but the High Court requires legal representation. Defendants may not be compelled to testify or confess guilt and may appeal a judgment. The law extends the above rights to all citizens.

Political Prisoners and Detainees

There were no reports of political prisoners or detainees.

Civil Judicial Procedures and Remedies

There is an independent and impartial judiciary with jurisdiction over civil matters. Individuals and organizations may freely access the court system to file lawsuits seeking cessation of human rights violations and recovery of damages. There were no regional human rights bodies where individuals and organizations may appeal adverse domestic decisions. In 2014, however, Senate Masupha launched a complaint over inheritance of her father's chieftainship at the African Commission on Human and People's Rights in Banjul, The Gambia (see section 6).

f. Arbitrary or Unlawful Interference with Privacy, Family, Home, or Correspondence

The constitution and laws prohibit arbitrary interference with privacy, family, home, and correspondence, and the government generally respected these prohibitions. Although search warrants are required under normal circumstances, the law provides police with the power to stop and search persons and vehicles as well as enter homes and other places without a warrant if the situation is life threatening or if there are other security concerns. The law states any police officer of the rank of inspector or above may search individuals or homes without a warrant.

Section 2. Respect for Civil Liberties, Including:

a. Freedom of Speech and Press

The constitution and law provide for freedom of speech, but the constitution does not explicitly mention freedom of the press. Media freedom deteriorated and was marked by several incidents, including intimidation of journalists by state security institutions, the shooting of an editor, and threats and legal action against the press.

Freedom of Speech and Expression: The law prohibits expressions of hatred or contempt for any person because of the person's race, ethnic affiliation, gender, disability, or color. The government did not arrest or convict anyone under the law. The NSS reportedly monitored political meetings.

Press and Media Freedoms: The law grants citizens the right to free expression, including obtaining and imparting information freely, but only as long as it does not interfere with "defense, public safety, public order, public morality, or public health."

The independent media were active and expressed a wide variety of views. Many media enterprises, however, relied on government advertising for revenue, making them vulnerable to government financial pressure. For example, in May a leaked and widely distributed Ministry of Finance internal memorandum revealed that staff were "no longer allowed to place departmental advertisements in *Lesotho Times*, *Public Eye*, and *Informative* newspapers until further notice." The newspapers contacted Minister of Finance Mamphono Khaketla, who claimed she had no knowledge of the memorandum despite it being drafted by her principal secretary and copying her. The ministry subsequently announced that the memorandum applied only to the Ministry of Finance and was issued because of limited government funding. Subsequently the three newspapers reported the government did not purchase any advertising for vacancies or tenders, although they received occasional government requests to purchase advertising to publicize government events or achievements.

Violence and Harassment: On June 23, police questioned *Lesotho Times* reporter Keiso Mohloboli and pressured her to reveal her sources following the publication of her article stating the government had offered LDF Commander Tlali Kamoli 40 million maloti ($2.8 million) to vacate his position. Police released her five hours later after she agreed to write a personal apology to Kamoli and the newspaper agreed to retract the story. The next day police detained Mohloboli again for questioning. The newspaper's editor, Lloyd Mutungamiri, a Zimbabwean national, accompanied her voluntarily. Police later released Mohloboli but kept the editor's passport for several days.

On July 9, Mutungamiri was shot in the face and arm by unknown gunmen while in a car attempting to enter his residence. He survived and was hospitalized under police guard for several days in Maseru before being transferred to a hospital in South Africa. Minister of Communications Khotso Letsatsi condemned the action and promised the government would work tirelessly to bring the perpetrators to justice but also strongly criticized the media for the way they handle "sensitive state information." At year's end authorities had not charged anyone.

On July 19, the publisher Basildon Peta's case for defamation of Kamoli was postponed after he failed to appear in court and his lawyer insisted that it was not safe for him to return to Lesotho.

One week later, fearing for her safety, *Lesotho Times* reporter Mohloboli also left the country.

Censorship or Content Restrictions: There were several instances of government censorship. For example, on November 10, nongovernment radio stations suddenly went off the air at the end of a live broadcast of a press conference where a faction of the prime minister's party (the DC) announced the party's withdrawal from the government's seven-party coalition. The Ministry of Communications manages the one radio transmission tower and in the past reportedly had cut broadcasts that might have been viewed as critical of the government. In this case it told the private stations the three-hour interruption in service resulted from technical issues related to a thunderstorm. The next morning, as parliament was opening after the political upheaval of the previous day and a two-week break, all radio stations that used the government transmission tower, including those that were government run, were off the air for "routine maintenance" but started broadcasting later in the morning after parliament had adjourned.

In August the president of the Democratic Congress Youth League (DCYL), the youth wing of the prime minister's party, went on government-owned Radio Lesotho and claimed the minister of finance was corrupt and had sought kickbacks for a large government tender. During the radio broadcast, Minister of Communications Khotso Letsatsi reportedly called the station and ordered it to halt the program. The station complied with no on-air explanation. Later a recording was leaked of a private conversation between the DCYL president and Minister Letsatsi, in which the minister explained the reason he had the show stopped was to prevent internal party disagreements from being broadcast in public.

Libel/Slander Laws: In order to avoid slander and libel lawsuits, some journalists practiced self-censorship. On June 27, the *Lesotho Times'* Zimbabwean publisher, Basildon Peta, was charged with unlawfully, intentionally, and seriously impairing the dignity of another and maliciously defaming the army commander following the publication of an anonymous satirical article suggesting that civilian authorities reported to him.

Internet Freedom

The government did not restrict or disrupt access to the internet or censor online content. In early November, however, the Lesotho Communications Authority requested in writing that the country's two mobile phone carriers and internet providers provide information on whether a temporary restriction of access to Facebook and Twitter usage was possible. The Media Institute of Southern Africa in Lesotho and the Consumer Protection Agency expressed serious concern about the possible implications of such a request.

There were no credible reports the government monitored private online communications without appropriate legal authority. The internet was not widely available and almost nonexistent in rural areas due to lack of communications infrastructure and high cost of access. According to the International Telecommunication Union, approximately 16 percent of the population had access to the internet in 2015.

Academic Freedom and Cultural Events

There were no government restrictions on academic freedom or cultural events.

In May unknown assailants reportedly attacked the home of National University of Lesotho (NUL) professor Mafa Sejanamane, who had been a vocal critic of the government. He heard gunshots followed by the sound of shattering windowpanes. Sejanamane and his daughter, the only two persons in the house at the time, hid until the morning. They later discovered six stones not usually found in the area, one inside the house and the rest outside the broken windows. The assailants had cut a security fence and entered through the opening. No one was hurt during the attack.

b. Freedom of Peaceful Assembly and Association

The constitution and law provide for freedom of assembly and association, but the law requires public meetings and procession organizers to obtain a permit seven days in advance. The government generally respected these rights if a permit was sought. Police prevented the September 5 and 6 NUL students' demonstration against the National Manpower Development Secretariat over unpaid allowances. Police asserted that the students had not applied for a permit to demonstrate, while students indicated they were only marching to Maseru to seek information on their student grants. On September 7, police reportedly assaulted students in off-campus residences. A police spokesperson denied the claim.

According to the *Sunday Express* newspaper, in a letter dated September 19, the Maseru Urban District Police Commissioner, Senior Superintendent Motlatsi Mapola refused to grant the students a permit for another march on September 27, citing concerns the procession would not be peaceful and encouraging them to schedule the protest for another date. The students appealed to Police Minister Monyane Moleleki, who overturned the decision and granted them a permit to march. On October 5, the commissioner of police and the Office of the Attorney General challenged the police minister's decision in court and lost. The march went ahead on October 6.

c. Freedom of Religion

See the Department of State's *International Religious Freedom Report* at www.state.gov/religiousfreedomreport/.

d. Freedom of Movement, Internally Displaced Persons, Protection of Refugees, and Stateless Persons

The constitution and law provide for freedom of internal movement, foreign travel, emigration, and repatriation, and the government generally respected these rights.

The government cooperated with the Office of the UN High Commissioner for Refugees and other humanitarian organizations in providing protection and assistance to refugees, asylum seekers, stateless persons, and other persons of concern.

Protection of Refugees

Access to Asylum: The law provides for the granting of asylum or refugee status, and the government has established a system for providing protection to refugees. The system was active and accessible.

Section 3. Freedom to Participate in the Political Process

The constitution and law provide citizens the ability to choose their government in free and fair periodic elections held by secret ballot and based on universal and equal suffrage.

Elections and Political Participation

Recent Elections: During the February 2015 national election, no single political party emerged the winner. The DC obtained 47 seats in the 120-seat National Assembly. It formed a seven-party, 65-seat coalition with the Lesotho Congress for Democracy (LCD), which had 12 seats; the Popular Front for Democracy, which had two seats; and the Marematlou Freedom Party, Basotho Congress Party, National Independent Party, and Lesotho People's Congress, each of which had one seat. The All Basotho Convention (ABC), which won 46 seats, and Basotho National Party with seven seats were ousted from power. The newly formed Reformed Congress of Lesotho, which broke away from the LCD shortly before elections, won two seats.

In March 2015 outgoing Prime Minister Motsoahae Thomas Thabane peacefully handed power over to DC party leader Pakalitha Mosisili. Mosisili had conceded power to Thabane following elections in 2012. Domestic and international observers characterized the 2015 election as peaceful and conducted in a credible, transparent, and professional manner. The election was called two years and three months early after clashes between police and LDF in 2014 led Thabane to flee the country. A SADC facilitation mission negotiated the snap election.

ABC leader Thabane, who was also the leader of the opposition, and the leaders of two other opposition parties fled the country in May 2015, citing security concerns. SADC encouraged Thabane and the other two leaders to return to Lesotho in part to facilitate constitutional and security sector reforms. Despite attempts by the prime minister to assuage Thabane's security concerns, none of the leaders had returned by year's end. Two ABC members of parliament had also fled the country, citing security concerns.

<u>Participation of Women and Minorities</u>: No laws prevent women or minorities from voting, serving as electoral monitors or otherwise participating in political life on the same basis as men or ethnic Basotho citizens. The law provides for the allocation of one-third of the seats in the municipal, urban, and community councils to women. The law also states a political party registered with the Independent Electoral Commission must facilitate the full participation of women, youth, and persons with disabilities. Party lists for the 40 proportional representation seats in the National Assembly must include equal numbers of women and men.

Women held several prominent positions in government. The speaker of the National Assembly was a woman, as was the chief justice, governor of the Central Bank of Lesotho, and the chief executive of the Lesotho Highlands Development Authority. Two women held the rank of colonel in the LDF.

More than 98 percent of the population is ethnic Basotho. There were no members of minority groups in the National Assembly, Senate, or cabinet.

Section 4. Corruption and Lack of Transparency in Government

The law provides criminal penalties for corruption by officials. The government did not implement the law effectively, however, and some officials reportedly engaged in corrupt practices with impunity.

<u>Corruption</u>: In July the DCYL accused then finance minister Mamphono Khaketla of corruption for awarding Bidvest, a South African company, a no-bid, multimillion dollar contract to manage the government's vehicle fleet for four years. The contract was initially bid as an open tender, and a local consortium claimed to have internal government documents identifying it as the preferred bidder. The consortium further claimed that Thabo Napo, a businessman believed to have a close personal relationship with the finance minister, had solicited from them a four million maloti ($286,000) bribe for the consortium to obtain the contract. The consortium said it declined to pay, the tender was canceled, and the contract awarded in a noncompetitive process to Bidvest.

On August 8, police reportedly questioned one of the consortium's directors, Letsatsi Mabona, on how he obtained the internal government tender evaluation report and then released him. On August 10, three members of the DCYL Executive Committee and six members of the consortium fled the country, claiming to have heard rumors that police were going to "torture them to death." Police denied the claims. They returned on August 22, and the consortium filed a commercial court case on August 28 challenging the award of the contract to Bidvest. Khaketla sued for defamation and held a press conference on September 14 denying the allegation of corruption.

<u>Financial Disclosure</u>: The law requires appointed and elected officials to disclose income and assets and prohibits false or misleading declarations. The declaration regime identifies which assets, liabilities, and other interests public officials must declare. Officials must file their declarations annually by April 30. The law provides for disciplinary measures and criminal penalties for failure to comply. The law does not require public declarations or that officials file declarations upon leaving office. The law mandates that the DCEO monitor and verify disclosures. The DCEO claimed it could not effectively implement the law because it lacked adequate resources.

During the year staff at some ministries declared their assets and potential conflicts of interest, but others did not. No ministers declared assets or conflicts of interest. Authorities did not question any declaration's veracity or impose sanctions.

<u>Public Access to Information</u>: The law does not provide for public access to government information. Some ministries made information available to the public but not according to any stated policy or procedure. The government put few of its publications online.

Section 5. Governmental Attitude Regarding International and Nongovernmental Investigation of Alleged Violations of Human Rights

A number of domestic and international human rights groups generally operated without government restriction, investigating and publishing their findings on human rights cases. According to some local NGOs, government officials were not cooperative and responsive to their views and accused NGOs of not being impartial. The government has never permitted the International Committee of the Red Cross to visit the LDF detainees.

The United Nations or Other International Bodies: Following former LDF commander Mahao's June 2015 killing, the government sought SADC support for an investigation. The result was the appointment of a nine-member SADC commission of inquiry to investigate the killing, alleged mutiny, and divisions within the LDF. Beginning in August 2015, the commission heard testimony from many high-ranking current and former government officials. The LDF, however, declined to provide the names of soldiers involved in the operation that led to Mahao's death or any operational details or answer questions about the alleged mutiny, arguing that would conflict with the court-martial. Commissioners expressed public frustration concerning LDF's refusal to cooperate. The prime minister initially declined to accept the commission's report during the January 18 SADC Double Troika Summit, citing a pending case filed by LDF Lieutenant Colonel Tefo Hashatsi. Hashatsi challenged the legitimacy of the commission and argued that it did not have a mandate to hear evidence in South Africa because it had been established under Lesotho law. Prime Minister Mosisili ultimately accepted the report and presented an expunged version to the parliament on February 8. On December 1, the government implemented the first of the commission's recommendations by retiring Lieutenant General Tlali Kamoli. On December 12, the government hosted a meeting with members of 16 political parties and a number of NGOs, but opposition parties walked out after stating the process could not go forward while their leaders remained in exile and claiming that the government was attempting to dictate the terms of reform rather than facilitate an inclusive process.

Government Human Rights Bodies: The independent Office of the Ombudsman appeared to function without government or political interference. The office was partially effective but constrained by a low level of public awareness and use of its services because its operations were limited to Maseru and it had insufficient staffing, financing, and equipment. The ombudsman intervened in response to requests involving nonpayment of death benefits by the Public Service Pension

Fund to beneficiaries. In November 2015 the minister of law and constitutional affairs introduced a bill in parliament establishing a human rights commission and on June 3, the king enacted the bill into law. Two NGOs, Development for Peace Education and the TRC, however, filed a constitutional court case on August 8 urging the court to declare the bill invalid on procedural grounds. They were specifically concerned the bill gave the prime minister too much power in appointing commission members. The government had not established the commission by year's end.

Section 6. Discrimination, Societal Abuses, and Trafficking in Persons

Women

<u>Rape and Domestic Violence</u>: The law criminalizes rape, including spousal rape, and domestic violence. Rape convictions carry a minimum sentence of 10 years' imprisonment. When informed, police generally enforced the law promptly and effectively; however, cases proceeded slowly in the judiciary. Sexual assault and rape were commonplace. Local and international NGOs reported that most incidents of sexual assault and rape went unreported. From December 2015 to August, the police Child and Gender Protection Unit (CGPU) received reports of 150 cases involving rape or sexual assault of children. Between January and March, the CGPU received 157 reports of all categories of sexual offenses, of which 79 were pending investigation and 44 pending prosecution. There were convictions in four cases and five were withdrawn. During the same period, the CGPU received 25 reports of sexual assault (a subcategory of sexual offenses). Seventeen were pending investigation, six were pending prosecution, and authorities obtained one conviction. From January to August, the Magistrate Court recorded 202 sexual offense cases involving 230 suspects. Sixty-five cases were completed and 52 suspects convicted. Police withdrew 10 cases, eight of which involved children, due to lack of evidence.

Domestic violence against women was widespread. The CGPU did not compile data on domestic violence. The LMPS included reports of domestic violence with assault data but did not break down the data by type of violence. Assault, domestic violence, and spousal abuse are criminal offenses, but authorities brought few cases to trial. The law does not mandate specific penalties, and judges have wide discretion in sentencing. Judges may authorize release of an offender with a warning, give a suspended sentence, or, depending on the severity of the assault, fine or imprison an offender.

Advocacy and awareness programs by the Office of the First Lady, CGPU, ministries, and Women and Law in Southern Africa (WLSA) changed public perceptions of violence against women and children by arguing that violence was unacceptable. The activities of local and regional organizations, other NGOs, and broadcast and print media campaigns bolstered these efforts. The government had one shelter in Maseru for abused women. The shelter offered psychosocial services but provided help only to women referred to it. The majority of victims did not know about the shelter. There was no hotline for victims.

<u>Other Harmful Traditional Practices</u>: There were reports of forced elopement, a customary practice whereby men abduct and rape girls or women with the intention of forcing them into marriage, but no estimate on its extent was available. When the perpetrator's family was wealthy, the victim's parents often reached a financial settlement rather than report the incident to police. According to the *Sunday Express* newspaper, the minister of education and training said that in Mokhotlong District, where the rate of school dropouts was highest, the abduction and killing of girls were most prevalent.

<u>Sexual Harassment</u>: The law criminalizes sexual harassment, indecent exposure, and sexual assault. Penalties for those convicted of sexual harassment are at the discretion of the court. Victims rarely reported sexual harassment. According to WLSA, sexual harassment in the textile sector increased. Police also believed sexual harassment to be widespread in the workplace and elsewhere. The CGPU prepared radio programs to raise public awareness of the problem.

<u>Reproductive Rights</u>: The law gives couples and individuals the right to decide the number, spacing, and timing of their children; manage their reproductive health; and have access to the information and means to do so, free from discrimination, coercion, and violence.

Social and cultural barriers, but no legal prohibitions, limited access to contraception and related services. There was access to modern contraception for a minimal fee; male and female condoms were readily available free of charge. Many international and local NGOs worked in partnership with the government to provide such services. The 2014 Lesotho Demographic and Health Survey (LDHS) revealed the contraceptive prevalence rate peaked among women at 71 percent between the ages of 35-39 and declined to 40 percent among women between ages 45 and 49. It observed a correlation between education, wealth, and contraceptive use; women with living children were more likely than those without living children to use contraceptives.

The 2014 LDHS reported the maternal mortality ratio was 1,024 per 100,000 live births, largely due to limitations in the country's health system. Although the ratio dropped slightly from 1,243 per 100,000 live births in 2009, the change was not statistically significant. According to the survey, 95 percent of women who gave birth in the five years before the survey, received antenatal care from a skilled provider for their most recent birth. Only 41 percent, however, had their first antenatal visit during the first trimester, and only 74 percent had the recommended four or more visits.

Discrimination: Except for inheritance rights, women enjoyed the same legal status and rights as men. The law prohibits discrimination against women in access to employment or credit, education, pay, housing, or in owning or managing businesses. The law prohibits discrimination against women under formal as well as customary or traditional law. Formal, but not customary, law protects inheritance, succession, and property rights. Civil law defers to customary law, which discriminates against women and girls as it pertains to inheritance. Customary law limits inheritance to male heirs only; it does not permit women or girls to inherit property. A woman married under civil law may contest inheritance rights in civil court.

Although the civil legal code does not recognize polygyny, a small minority practiced it under customary law.

Under the civil legal system, women have the right to make a will and sue for divorce. To have legal standing in civil court, a couple must register a customary law marriage in the civil system.

In April 2014 the Court of Appeal unanimously upheld the Constitutional Court's 2013 decision to dismiss Senate Masupha's suit to inherit her father's title and estate as principal chief of Teyateyaneng, ending her four-year legal battle. The Court of Appeal upheld male primogeniture. In October 2014 Masupha launched a complaint at the African Commission on Human and People's Rights. According to the Ministry of Law and Constitutional Affairs, the commission had not ruled on admissibility of the case.

Promoting the rights of women is among the responsibilities of the Ministry of Gender, Youth, and Sports. It supported efforts by women's groups to sensitize society to respect the status and rights of women.

Children

Birth Registration: According to the constitution, birth within the country's territory confers citizenship. According to the Office of National Identity and Civil Registry (NICR) in the Ministry of Home Affairs, all births in hospitals and local clinics are registered. Births of children in private homes are reported to the offices of local chiefs, which provide letters to parents for presentation to the NICR for issuance of birth certificates. The law stipulates registration within three months of birth but allows up to one year without penalty. After one year a nominal fee of 2.50 maloti ($0.18) is charged. In 2013 the Ministry of Home Affairs began implementing the National Identity Cards Act of 2011 by issuing identity cards to citizens over age 16. Applicants for these cards and electronic passports must submit new birth certificates with added security features.

Education: By law primary education, which goes through grade seven, is universal, compulsory, and tuition-free beginning at age six. The law leaves open the age by which children must complete grade seven; however, the Ministry of Education set the maximum age for free primary education at 13. Secondary education is not free, but the government offered scholarships for orphans and other vulnerable children. Authorities may impose a fine of not less than 1,000 maloti ($71) or imprisonment on a parent whose child failed to attend school regularly. There were no reports of police fining or imprisoning parents.

According to the UN Children's Fund (UNICEF), many children did not attend school. The problem was particularly prevalent in rural areas, where there were few schools. Attending school regularly was most difficult for orphans and other vulnerable children, those involved in supporting their families through subsistence activities, or those whose families could not afford fees for the purchase of uniforms, books, and other school materials.

Child Abuse: While the law prohibits child abuse, it was nevertheless a problem, especially for orphans and other vulnerable children. Neglect, common assault, sexual assault, and forced elopement--a customary practice of abducting a girl with the intention of marrying her without her consent--occurred.

With branches in all 10 districts, the CGPU led the government's efforts to combat child abuse; however, lack of resources limited its effectiveness. The CGPU sought to address sexual and physical abuse, neglect, and abandonment of children, and protection of the property rights of orphans. It also advocated changing cultural norms that encourage forced elopement.

The Maseru Magistrate's Court had a children's court as part of a government initiative to protect children's rights.

There were no media reports of violence at traditional initiation schools. Attended mainly by rural youth, these schools used traditional rituals to initiate teenage boys into manhood. While the activities of these initiation schools were secret, in years past media reported violence against students, teachers, and members of surrounding communities.

Early and Forced Marriage: The Children's Protection and Welfare Act defines a child as a person under age 18. Under the Marriage Act of 1974, however, a girl can marry at age 16, while a boy can do so at age 18. The act states that "if the girl is 16 years of age, but is not yet 21, parental consent is required" for marriage. Customary law does not set a minimum age for marriage. According to UN Population Fund data collected between 2000 and 2011, an estimated 19 percent of women between the ages of 20 and 24 were married before age 18. Starting in June the minister of social development held public gatherings in five districts in a campaign to end child marriage.

Sexual Exploitation of Children: The law sets the minimum age for consensual sex at 18. Anyone who commits an offense related to the commercial sexual exploitation of children is liable to imprisonment for a period of not less than 10 years. Child pornography carries a similar sentence. An antitrafficking in persons law criminalizes trafficking of children or adults for the purposes of sexual or physical exploitation and abuse. Offenders convicted of trafficking children into prostitution are liable to a fine of two million maloti ($142,857) or life imprisonment. The court may apply the death penalty if a knowingly HIV-positive perpetrator sexually assaults a child who becomes infected. Authorities enforced the law.

Child prostitution was a problem. Impoverished young girls and boys, many of whom were orphans, moved to urban areas to engage in prostitution. After being fraudulently recruited with promises of better opportunities, Basotho girls were also exploited in prostitution in South Africa. UNICEF and government officials agreed that while the numbers remained small, the commercial sexual exploitation of children was a growing problem.

International Child Abductions: The country is a party to the 1980 Hague Convention on the Civil Aspects of International Child Abduction. See the

Department of State's *Annual Report on International Parental Child Abduction* at travel.state.gov/content/childabduction/en/legal/compliance.html.

Anti-Semitism

There was a small Jewish community. There were no reports of anti-Semitic acts.

Trafficking in Persons

See the Department of State's *Trafficking in Persons Report* at www.state.gov/j/tip/rls/tiprpt/.

Persons with Disabilities

The constitution and law prohibit discrimination against persons with disabilities in employment, education, access to health care, or the provision of other state services. The constitution does not refer to specific disabilities or to access to air travel and other transportation. The labor code and Public Service Act do not specifically provide for meaningful access to employment in both the private and public sectors by persons with disabilities. The national disability policy establishes a framework for inclusion of persons with disabilities in poverty reduction and social development programs, but by year's end, the government had not incorporated objectives or guidelines for the implementation of these programs. The Association of the Disabled promoted the rights and needs of persons with disabilities.

Persons with disabilities were disadvantaged regarding access to public buildings, employment, education, air travel, and other transportation, information and communications, and health care. Laws and regulations stipulate that persons with disabilities should have access to public buildings. Public buildings completed after 1995 generally complied with the law, but many older buildings remained inaccessible. There was no accommodation for persons with disabilities in air or other transportation. The Lesotho National Federation of Organizations of the Disabled complained about the limited budget for sign language interpreters in the judicial system, resulting in case postponements. Braille and JAWS (computer software used by persons with vision disabilities) were not widely available. Service providers in the government or private sector did not provide sign language interpreters (except Lesotho Television--see below), so hearing-disabled persons who sign could not access state services. There were limited facilities for training persons with disabilities. Children with physical disabilities attended school; however, facilities to accommodate them in primary, secondary, and higher education were limited. One school accommodated specifically children with vision disabilities, two schools accommodated specifically children with hearing and speech disabilities, and two schools accommodated specifically children with intellectual disabilities and multiple disabilities. An additional 243 schools integrated children with disabilities into their general student population. Although the government did not effectively implement laws that provide for persons with disabilities to have access to information and communications, in 2013 Lesotho Television introduced sign language interpretation during its daily news broadcast. On August 18, the Ministry of Social Development held a workshop for banking institutions and insurance companies. The director of disability services urged the institutions to review their policies to accommodate the needs of persons with disabilities.

There were no reports of persons with disabilities being abused in a prison, school, or mental health facility. According to the Lesotho National Federation of Organizations of the Disabled, however, such abuse likely occurred regularly but went unreported.

Acts of Violence, Discrimination, and Other Abuses Based on Sexual Orientation and Gender Identity

The law prohibits consensual sexual relations between men, but authorities did not enforce it. The law is silent on consensual sex between women. Lesbian, gay, bisexual, transgender, and intersex (LGBTI) persons faced societal discrimination and official insensitivity to this discrimination. LGBTI rights groups complained of discrimination in access to health care and participation in religious activities.

The law prohibits discrimination attributable to sex; it does not explicitly forbid discrimination against LGBTI. Matrix, an LGBTI advocacy and support group, had no reports of employment discrimination from its members. Same-sex sexual relationships were taboo in society and not openly discussed. While there were no assaults reported, LGBTI persons often did not report incidents of violence due to fear of stigma.

Matrix operated freely and had members in all 10 districts. It reported having a good working relationship with the LMPS. For instance, in December 2015 the brothers of a woman who identified herself as a lesbian forced her out of her home when they discovered her sexual identity. She took the matter to police, who intervened, and the brothers allowed her to return home.

Matrix engaged in public outreach through film screenings, radio programs, public gatherings, and social media. On May 21, Matrix organized the third International Day Against Homophobia and Transphobia march. Approximately 200 individuals, mainly family and friends of LGBTI persons, marched peacefully and without incident from Lakeside (city outskirts) to Central Park in Maseru. Matrix representatives noted police officers escorting the march were generally supportive, which they attributed to Matrix's previous outreach efforts to the LMPS. Matrix for several months also had an electronic billboard advertisement in central Maseru supporting LGBTI rights.

Addressing the media in June following the UN General Assembly High-Level Meeting on HIV/AIDS, Deputy Prime Minister Mothetjoa Metsing said the government would look into decriminalizing same-sex relationships to stop the spread of HIV. This was the first pronouncement made by a high-level government official on the issue.

HIV and AIDS Social Stigma

Access to antiretroviral (ARV) therapy increased, with 143,371 persons receiving treatment, according to the Ministry of Health April to June report. This number remained below national targets and was lower than needed to control the epidemic in line with UNAIDS' (UN AIDS program) 90/90/90 targets. On April 14, the country adopted a "test and treat" approach whereby all HIV-positive individuals are immediately eligible to enroll for treatment.

In the most recent (2014) LDHS, a majority of women and men reported having tolerant attitudes toward HIV-positive relatives, teachers, and shopkeepers. More than 90 percent stated they would be willing to care for HIV-positive members of their families, 92 percent of women and 81 percent of men would accept HIV-positive female teachers in the classroom, and 88 percent of women and 80 percent of men would buy fresh fruits or vegetables from a vendor known to be HIV-positive. Far fewer women and men indicated they would disclose that a family member was infected with HIV/AIDS (56 percent of women and 53 percent of men).

Almost 94 percent of women accessing antenatal care were tested for HIV; of that number, 24 percent were HIV-positive. Of the women who tested positive, 91 percent received ARV prophylaxis or highly active antiviral therapy to protect both mother and child.

The Lesotho Network of People Living with HIV and AIDS (LENEPWA)
Executive Director Boshepha Ranthithi stated that HIV/AIDS stigma could not be
comprehensively addressed due to the 2011 closure of the National AIDS
Commission and the lack of a law specifically addressing the problem.
Widespread discrimination and stigma persisted. The government reestablished
the commission in December 2015.

Other Societal Violence or Discrimination

The media reported killing of elderly persons, primarily in connection with
accusations of witchcraft, and sporadic incidents of mob violence targeting
suspected criminals. For example, in April a mob at Ha Tsolo, Maseru, assaulted
and burned to death a murder and burglary suspect. They also assaulted another
suspect, but police rescued him as the mob attempted to burn him.

The media reported a spate of retaliatory killings among local accordion music
artists fighting over provocative lyrics that insulted other artists in Maseru,
Mafeteng, and Mohale's Hoek districts.

Section 7. Worker Rights

a. Freedom of Association and the Right to Collective Bargaining

By law workers in the private sector have the right to join and form trade unions of
their own choosing without prior authorization or excessive bureaucratic
requirements. The law prohibits civil servants and police from joining or forming
unions but allows them to form staff associations for collective bargaining and
promoting ethical conduct of their members. All trade unions must register with
the Registrar of Trade Unions. The law allows unions to conduct their activities
without interference.

The law provides for a limited right to strike. In the private sector, the law requires
workers and employers to follow a series of procedures designed to resolve
disputes before the Directorate of Dispute Prevention and Resolution, an
independent government body, authorizes a strike. The law does not permit civil
servants to strike.

The law protects collective bargaining and places no restrictions on it. The law
permits unions to bargain for wages above the minimum wage. Government

approval is not required for collective agreements to be valid. Under the law regulating civil servants, the Public Service Joint Advisory Council provides for due process and protects civil servants' rights. The council consists of an equal number of members appointed by the minister of public service and members of any association representing at least 50 percent of civil servants. The council concludes and enforces collective bargaining agreements, prevents and resolves disputes, and provides procedures for dealing with general grievances. Furthermore, the Public Service Tribunal handles appeals brought by civil servants or their associations.

The law prohibits antiunion discrimination and other employer interference in union functions. The law provides for reinstatement of workers dismissed for union activity. The law does not exclude particular groups of workers from relevant legal protections.

The government enforces applicable laws with cases typically resolved within one or two months. A minority of cases lodged with the Department of Labor, a division within the Ministry of Labor and Employment, the Directorate of Dispute Prevention and Resolution (DDPR), and the Labor Court took up to nine months to be resolved. It was rare for a case to take longer than nine months, even though the labor court had only one judge and one labor court register. The DDPR had seven arbitrators nationwide with three vacant positions. A decrease in the number of arbitrators was not a binding constraint as the number of arbitration cases had declined due to efficient and effective dispute prevention activities to educate both employers and employees.

Employers generally supported freedom of association and collective bargaining. Although factory workers have bargaining power, only some workers exercised the right to bargain collectively. This is because the law requires any union entering into negotiations with management to represent 50 percent of workers, and only a few factories met that condition. In May 2015 the Factory Workers Union (Fawu), the Lesotho Clothing and Allied Workers Union, and the National Union of Textile Workers merged to form the Independent Democratic Union of Lesotho to strengthen their bargaining power. The National Clothing Textile and Allied Workers Union, which separated from Fawu, remained blacklisted by employers who alleged the founders had deliberately incited labor strikes. All worker organizations were independent of the government and political parties except the Lesotho Workers Party-affiliated Factory Workers Union. Most unions focused on organizing apparel workers.

Factory owners in the apparel industry were generally willing to bargain collectively on wages and working conditions, but only with trade unions that represented at least 50 percent of workers. Factory decisions concerning labor disputes are determined by companies' headquarters, which are usually located overseas. In the retail sector, employers generally respected freedom to associate and the right to bargain collectively, although retail unions complained employers commonly appealed labor court rulings to delay implementation of the rulings.

The International Labor Organization's Better Work Lesotho (BWL) program, which aims to improve compliance with national labor laws and international labor standards within the apparel industry, worked to increase understanding of national labor law and internationally recognized core labor standards. The program ended in June.

Staff at the Avani Lesotho Hotel (Lesotho Sun at the beginning of the strike) were on strike from December 2014 to the end of 2015 over demands for a 14 percent salary increase. Following the end of the strike, employees filed a court case against their employer after they failed to reach a mutual agreement on salaries and working conditions.

In the public sector, while both police and civil servants had associations, no single association represented at least 50 percent of civil servants. According to the Lesotho Public Servants Staff Association (LEPSSA), approximately 34 percent of civil servants belonged to the association. LEPSSA reported most civil servants did not register for the association because they were unaware of it. This low rate of participation made it difficult for LEPSSA to engage with the government on workers' rights problems.

Despite the law against antiunion discrimination, reinstatement was rarely enforced.

b. Prohibition of Forced or Compulsory Labor

The law prohibits all forms of forced or compulsory labor, but the government did not effectively enforce the applicable law. Police reported that inadequate resources hampered their investigations and remediation efforts, although penalties for violations, including two million maloti ($142,857) or 25 years' imprisonment, were sufficient to deter violations.

The CGPU conducted community outreach on forced labor through community gatherings, lectures, workshops, and radio programs. The newly established Human Trafficking Unit of the police targeted high schools to raise awareness of human trafficking and other forms of forced labor. Police reported one conviction for human trafficking, that of a Chinese man who sexually exploited a Chinese woman. The court sentenced the suspect to 15 years in prison with 10 years suspended. In another case a Nigerian man was accused of forcing another Nigerian man to build a house without pay. According to the CGPU, the case was initially addressed as a civil case. The victim, however, reported the nonpayment to the police, and they opened a trafficking-in-persons case, although the accused had not been formally charged and remained free. In a third case, involving a Kenyan man accused of forcing a Kenyan woman to work without pay as a hairdresser, police continued to investigate it as a potential case of human trafficking.

See the Department of State's *Trafficking in Persons Report* at www.state.gov/j/tip/rls/tiprpt/.

c. Prohibition of Child Labor and Minimum Age for Employment

The law defines the legal minimum age for employment as 15 years, or 18 for hazardous employment. Hazardous work includes mining and quarrying; carrying heavy loads; manufacturing where chemicals are produced or used; working in places where machines are used, or in places such as bars, hotels, and places of entertainment where a person may be exposed to immoral behavior; herding; and producing or distributing tobacco. While the legal minimum age for employment is 15 years, the law also provides that free and compulsory primary school be completed at age 13, two years before a child is legally allowed to work. The law does not prohibit the use, procuring, or offering of a child under age 18 for illicit activities (with the exception of commercial sexual exploitation of children, which is punishable by a fine of up to 30,000 maloti ($2,143) and 30 months' imprisonment). Any employer who breaches these provisions is liable to a fine, imprisonment, or both. Penalties for violation of the minimum age provisions include a fine not exceeding 20,000 maloti ($1,429) or imprisonment not exceeding 20 months. While the law protects children working in the informal economy, it excludes self-employed children from relevant legal protections.

The government did not effectively enforce minimum age laws for employment outside the formal economy, since scarce resources hindered labor inspections. The Ministry of Labor and Employment and the CGPU investigated cases of working children. The ministry had only two child labor inspectors, and 32 labor inspectors who did not specifically focus on child labor. There was one reported case of child labor, that of a 13-year-old boy employed as a herdboy.

Authorities did not prosecute any cases of child labor. Penalties for violations, including a fine not exceeding 20,000 maloti ($1,429) or imprisonment for a period not exceeding 20 months, were sufficient to deter violations.

In 2015 the government approved the guidelines for herdboys, which make a distinction between the concepts of "child work"--work that is not harmful and is acceptable as part of socialization--and "child labor"--those forms of work that are hazardous and exploitative. The guidelines apply to children below 18 years of age and strictly prohibit the engagement of children at a cattle post, the huts where herders stay when in remote mountain rangelands. Herding is considered illegal child labor only if herding deprives herdboys of the opportunity to attend school, obliges them to leave school prematurely, or requires them to combine school attendance with excessively long hours and difficult working conditions. The highest estimated percentage of working children was in herding. According to the Monna-ka-Khomo Herdboys Association, the literacy rate among herdboys was improving due to the implementation of the Education Act requiring the enrollment of six-year-old children in primary school. In addition, the NGO Sentebale, through its Herdboy Education Program, trained 10 herdboys, who completed a literacy and numeracy curriculum.

The Ministry of Labor and Employment completed approximately 965 labor inspections between April and September.

The Ministry of Labor and Employment and the CGPU continued to disseminate information on prevention of child labor as part of their other programs. To commemorate World Day Against Child Labor, the government conducted training for District Child Protection Teams in five districts; held radio talk shows; issued press statements; and organized 17 public gatherings to raise awareness about laws and regulations on child labor, which drew 137 attendees, 124 of whom were women, in five districts.

The most recent data available from the Bureau of Statistics, the 2011 Household Budget Survey, reported 3.5 percent of children ages six to 14 participated in economic activities; this statistic did not include children aiding their families or others without compensation. In its most recent report in 2014, UNICEF estimated 23 percent of children between ages five and 14 were working. Two-thirds of these children were engaged in subsistence farming, while the rest were engaged mainly in domestic service. Child labor was higher among boys (86.6 percent of child workers) than among girls (13.4 percent). The report was based on 2004 data provided by the Ministry of Labor and Employment.

See the Department of Labor's *Findings on the Worst Forms of Child Labor* at www.dol.gov/ilab/reports/child-labor/findings/.

d. Discrimination with Respect to Employment and Occupation

The labor code prohibits discrimination regarding race, color, sex, marital status, religion, political opinion, national extraction or social origin, and HIV/AIDS status, but it does not explicitly prohibit discrimination based on disability. There is no provision for equal pay for equal work.

Despite the law prohibiting gender-based discrimination in employment and occupation, such discrimination occurred. According to WLSA, there was no legal basis for discrimination against women in employment, business, and access to credit, although social barriers to equality remained. Both men and women reported that hiring practices often aligned with gender, with men preferentially selected for certain positions (such as mechanics) and women preferentially selected for other positions (such as sewing machine operators). In general, working conditions, while sometimes poor, were the same for both men and women.

A 2013 study by LENEPWA found substantial discrimination in employment and occupation against those who are HIV-positive (see section 6). The Ministry of Labor and Employment, however, did not report any cases during the year of such discrimination against those who were HIV-positive. The law prohibits such discrimination.

Migrant workers enjoy the same legal protections, wages, and working conditions as citizens.

e. Acceptable Conditions of Work

There is a sector-specific national minimum wage and a general minimum wage. The general minimum monthly wage varied from 1,213 maloti ($86.64) to 1,324 maloti ($94.57). The Lesotho Bureau of Statistics official estimate for the poverty income level was 246.60 maloti ($17.61) per month. Minimum wage provisions do not cover significant portions of the workforce. Labor laws do not cover workers in agriculture or other informal sectors.

The law stipulates standards for hours of work, including a maximum 45-hour workweek, a weekly rest period of at least 24 hours, a daily minimum rest period of one hour, at least 12 days of paid leave per year, paid sick leave, and public holidays. Required overtime is legal as long as overtime wages for work in excess of the standard 45-hour workweek are paid. The maximum overtime allowed is 11 hours per week; however, there are exemptions under special circumstances. The laws require the premium pay for overtime be at a rate not less than 125 percent of the employee's normal wage; any employer who requires excessive compulsory overtime is liable to a fine, imprisonment, or both.

The law empowers the Ministry of Labor and Employment to issue regulations on occupational health and safety standards. The law requires employers to provide adequate light, ventilation, and sanitary facilities for employees and to install and maintain machinery in a manner that minimizes injury. It also requires each employer to have a registered health and safety officer. Employers must provide first aid kits, safety equipment, and protective clothing. The law also provides for a compensation system for industrial injuries and diseases related to employment. Penalties for violations--not exceeding 200 maloti ($14.29) or up to six months' imprisonment--were insufficient to deter violations. The commissioner of labor is responsible for investigating allegations of labor law violations.

Labor inspectors worked in all districts and generally conducted unannounced inspections of a random sample of workplaces on a weekly basis. Businesses operating in the formal sector, including the apparel industry, were subject to more enforcement than businesses operating in the informal sector. The ministry began domesticating International Labor Organization Recommendation 204 to make the informal sector liable for inspection. The ministry's inspectorate reported employers, particularly in the security, transport, and construction sectors, did not always observe the minimum wage and hours of work laws. Many locally owned businesses did not keep employees' records to facilitate labor inspections as required by law. Smaller employers failed to establish safety committees, did not have complete first aid kits, and did not provide protective clothing. With the exception of the mining industry, employers' compliance with health and safety regulations generally was low. According to the Ministry of Labor and Employment, noncompliance with the health and safety regulations increased especially in construction, where there was an increasing frequency of fatal accidents. The BWL also reported some employers paid workers less than required by law for overtime work.

Trade union representatives described textile-sector working conditions as poor or even harsh but not dangerous. Union officials stated most textile factories were in prefabricated metal buildings. Unions reported few examples of dangerous health hazards but noted most factories had improper ventilation. Third-party auditors hired by foreign textile buyers conducted spot checks on many exporting factories, customarily sought labor's input, and briefed the unions on their findings. Unions believed the third-party auditors kept factory owners in line with health and safety regulations. Unions also mentioned compliance with labor law and labor standards was much higher at factories enrolled in the BWL program.

Many workplace policies covered employees with HIV/AIDS. Some of the larger factories maintained health services at the workplace. Where factories did not provide health care, workers had the right to access services at public health centers. Employers provided space for employee examinations and time off for employees to see doctors, receive counseling, and participate in educational and antistigma programs.

The Ministry of Labor and Employment is responsible for enforcing these laws and standards but limited budget resources constrained enforcement efforts. Inspections did not cover agricultural and other informal sectors, which employed most workers. The ministry estimated a significant number of workers were in the informal economy, although there was no reliable data on the number of such workers. The ministry's inspectorate noted penalties were not sufficient to deter violations. The BWL supported ministry inspection efforts by providing examples of crucial noncompliance and inconsistent labor law application to ensure that inspectors raised them with employers. The BWL also shared experiences and assessment findings with the ministry on a regular basis with a view to work toward industry-wide improvements.

The Ministry of Labor and Employment received 14 reports of workplace fatalities and accidents, many of which occurred in the textile industry. Ministry representatives indicated underreporting was a possibility.

Working conditions for foreign or migrant workers were similar to those of residents.

The law does not explicitly provide that workers can remove themselves from situations that endangered health or safety without jeopardy to their employment. Nevertheless, sections of the code on safety in the workplace and dismissal imply such a dismissal would be illegal. Authorities protected employees when violations of the law were reported.

www.ingramcontent.com/pod-product-compliance
Lightning Source LLC
Chambersburg PA
CBHW081256250726
48654CB00012B/1633